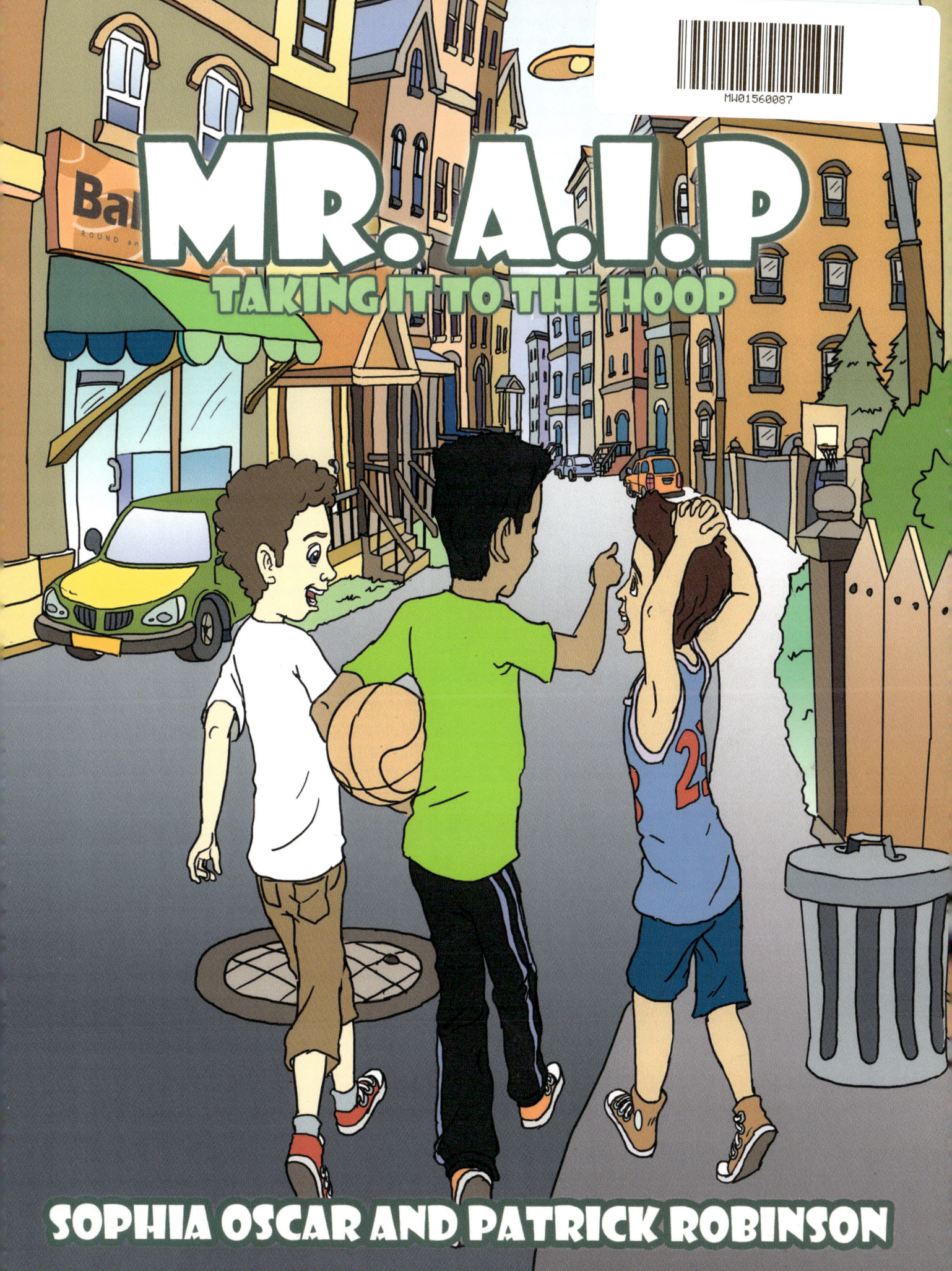

AuthorHouse™
1663 Liberty Drive
Bloomington, IN 47403
www.authorhouse.com
Phone: 1-800-839-8640

© 2011 Sophia Oscar and Patrick Robinson. All Rights Reserved.

No part of this book may be reproduced, stored in a retrieval system,
or transmitted by any means without the written permission of the author.

First published by AuthorHouse 05/18/2011

ISBN: 978-1-4634-1407-8 (sc)

Library of Congress Control Number: 2011908538

Printed in the United States of America

Any people depicted in stock imagery provided by Thinkstock are models,
and such images are being used for illustrative purposes only.
Certain stock imagery © Thinkstock.

This book is printed on acid-free paper.

Because of the dynamic nature of the Internet, any web addresses or links contained in this book may have changed since publication and may no longer be valid. The views expressed in this work are solely those of the author and do not necessarily reflect the views of the publisher, and the publisher hereby disclaims any responsibility for them.

It was a bright and sunny Saturday morning- the first day of summer. Nine year old Pat couldn't wait to go to the park and play basketball with his two best friends Chucky and Larry. "Mom, can I go to the park to play basketball with Chucky and Larry?" said Pat with excitement. "Sure you can pumpkin, after you finish your breakfast," his mother said. Pat finished his breakfast as fast as he could. He knew Chucky and Larry would be waiting for him outside.

When Pat opened his front door, Chucky and Larry were waiting on his front steps. "Hey Pat are you ready to go to the park," said Larry. "Yes, I have been waiting for this day all school year," said Pat. "Well, what are we waiting for? Let's go!" said Chucky.

The three boys continued down the street to the park where they were going to meet the other neighborhood kids. Pat, Chucky, and Larry always played on a team together but could never seem to win a game. "We're going to beat them this year," said Pat. "Yeah, we sure are," said Chucky. "I don't know guys... those kids are pretty good and we are probably going to lose like we do every summer," said Larry.

Pat, Chucky, and Larry gave it their all to try and win the game. Pat was missing a lot of his jump shots; Chucky was not doing a good job of playing defense; and Larry would lose the ball every time it was in his hands. Once again, the neighborhood boys defeated Pat, Chucky, and Larry. The three boys were feeling very disappointed and sad, so they decided to go back home.

Pat, Chucky, and Larry sat on the steps of Pat's house and talked about what a terrible game they played. "I don't think I want to play basketball anymore," Larry said. "I'm just not a good player." Larry had a gloomy look on his face. "We lose every time. We should just give up" said Chucky with his head hung low.

All of a sudden the boys felt a strong blow of wind and out appeared a man with a pink cape and green tights. "Wow! Who are you?" shouted Pat. "I'm Mr. A.I.P" said the man in the cape. "And I'm here to motivate you boys". Mr. A.I.P. stood up tall with confidence. He appeared to be some kind of superhero. "Are you a superhero?" Chucky asked. "I sure am" said Mr.A.I.P. "What does A.I.P. stand for?" asked Larry. Mr. A.I.P. smiled at the boys. "Anything Is Possible" he said.

The boys sat and stared at Mr. A.I.P in amazement while Mr. A.I.P. explained to them why he appeared at their steps. "I overheard you boys talking about giving up on basketball," said Mr. A.I.P. "I also heard you say you will never win a game against the neighborhood boys." Gazing at Mr. A.I.P, the boys continued to listen. "Well I'm here to tell you that Anything Is Possible, A.I.P." "You can become a good basketball player and beat the neighborhood boys." "All you have to do is follow three simple rules to become a great basketball player."

There was a pause; Pat's face lit up as he waited anxiously to hear Mr. A.I.P's three simple rules. "Rule number one: Think positive, Rule number two: Give it one hundred percent, and Rule number three: Practice, practice, practice," said Mr. A.I.P. Suddenly Mr. A.I.P. flew into the sky and disappeared.

The next day Pat, Chucky, and Larry woke up early to practice their basketball skills. They dribbled, they passed, and they practiced working as a team. The boys practiced every day for one week. Saturday was the day they were going to come face to face with the neighborhood boys and play them once again. They remembered the words Mr. A.I.P told them. Anything Is Possible, Anything Is Possible, Anything Is Possible. Pat, Chucky, and Larry were determined to become the best basketball players in the neighborhood.

Saturday came around and the boys were ready to go back to the park to play against the neighborhood boys. They were certain their hard work and hours of practicing would pay off. "We are going to win today," said Pat. "We are going to play our hardest," Chucky said. "Yeah, and we are going to do everything we practiced as a team," said Larry. Pat, Chucky, and Larry won their first game against the neighborhood boys. They jumped for joy after the game.

The three boys were so excited about their victory that they decided to treat themselves to some ice-cream. While sitting on the front steps of Pat's house they felt a strong blow of wind and there appeared Mr. A.I.P. "Hey! Mr. A.I.P we won our first game!" exclaimed Chucky. "I know you boys won your game and that is why I am here to congratulate you," said Mr. A.I.P. "I told you Anything Is Possible and that you could do it!"

The boys were grateful to Mr. A.I.P. "Thanks Mr. A.I.P.! Your advice gave us the motivation not to give up on basketball and become better players," said Pat. "When you feel like giving up or if you are having doubts, just remember those three simple words, Anything Is Possible" said Mr. A.I.P as he flew away into the sky.

THE END

CPSIA information can be obtained
at www.ICGtesting.com
233758LV00006B